THE EUCHARIST

ALCUIN CLUB MANUALS
No. 1

THE EUCHARIST

MICHAEL PERHAM

Second Edition, revised and reset

ALCUIN CLUB/SPCK

First published in 1978
for the Alcuin Club
Second edition,
revised and reset, 1981
SPCK
Holy Trinity Church
Marylebone Road
London NW1 4DU

ISBN 0 281 03836 8

Printed in Great Britain by
Spottiswoode Ballantyne Ltd.
Colchester and London

Contents

Preface to the First Edition

The year 1967 saw not only the authorisation of *Alternative Services Second Series An Order of Holy Communion* but also the publication of a useful booklet by John Wilkinson entitled *Eucharist for Experiment*, published by the Church Union. It sought to explain what was then a new and unfamiliar service which seemed not far short of revolutionary to many of those who encountered it for the first time. Ten years later, Series 2 is often regarded as 'old-fashioned'. Indeed the original intention was that by now it should have ceased to be available as one of the legal alternatives. Series 3 has taken a place alongside it, a similar service, save in its language, and far richer in seasonal material, as well as being recognisably the result of lessons learnt from the mistakes of Series 2. More recently Series 1 and 2 Revised presents a service that is much like Series 2, and certainly employs the more traditional language, but includes many of the Series 3 improvements.

The decade since 1967 has witnessed a revolution in the ways Anglicans do the liturgy. Some of the things that John Wilkinson proposed tentatively ten years ago are now accepted practice, and some of what he wrote, even that short time ago, is now dated. In the intervening years, the clergy have not received as much help as some of them would have liked with the ceremonial details of the new rites. Many of them have realised that the way they learnt to celebrate the Eucharist, though well suited to the Prayer Book rite facing east, has many disadvantages with the new liturgies and especially with a Eucharist facing the people. They have been trying to impose impossible rubrics on to the new rites. Or else they have done as some Anglicans have done before, and tried to adapt the current Roman rubrics to current Anglican liturgies. This has not been a very happy experiment, for, though Series 3 and *Ordo Missae* have many similarities, the liturgical insights behind the new rites are not at all points the same. This booklet is designed to meet this need to reorder the ceremonial of the service to fit the new rites.

The booklet is written principally with Series 3 in mind, but a good deal of reference is also made to Series 2 and also to Series 1 and 2 Revised, though with the latter rite it attempts to deal only with the alternatives in that rite that are similar to 3 and 2.

Some of the ideas in this booklet are drawn from John Wilkinson's booklet and some from a valuable booklet entitled *The Presentation of the Eucharist*, produced in 1971 by a joint working party of the Liturgical Commission and the Council for the Care of Churches. Those who seek further explanation of the theological and liturgical presuppositions of what follows will do well to turn to *The Eucharist Today*, edited by Ronald Jasper, and published in 1974 by SPCK.

Like John Wilkinson's *Eucharist for Experiment*, this booklet concludes with a detailed section on ceremonial, including a simple set of ceremonial directions for clergy and servers at a sung Eucharist. With a little adaptation, it should prove suitable for use in most churches.

I am deeply grateful to the Revd Dr Geoffrey Cuming for his advice and encouragement in the writing of this booklet. Without him the task would not have been undertaken or the effort sustained. Thanks are also due to the Dean of York, the Archdeacon of Hackney, the Revd A. M. Haig, the Revd Dr P. F. Bradshaw, and Canon J. D. C. Fisher, all of whom made helpful suggestions. Since not all their suggestions were heeded, the faults remain mine and mine alone. I also acknowledge my debt to the clergy and people of St Mary's, Addington, Croydon, who must sometimes feel as if they were being used as liturgical 'guinea-pigs', but who enable me to experience again and again the joy of celebrating the Eucharist.

Addington 1978   MICHAEL PERHAM

Preface to the Second Edition

The publication in November 1980 of the Alternative Service Book, and the inclusion within it of Rite A as the normative modern language Eucharistic liturgy of the Church of England, has provided good reason to revise this book quite extensively before the publication of the second edition.

The first edition was based on the requirements of Series 3, with reference also to Series 2 and Series 1 & 2 Revised. The text of this book has been modified and revised chiefly with Rite A in mind, but Series 3 continues to be considered, as does 1 & 2 Revised (now in a marginally revised form found as Rite B in the ASB). Series 2, almost superseded by Rite B, is not included in this new edition. Some sections of this book remain almost unaltered, but others have been extensively rewritten.

In addition to the books mentioned in the preface to the first edition, reference must be made to *The Alternative Service Book 1980: A Commentary by the Liturgical Commission*, published at the same time as the ASB, by the Church Information Office. Commended by the Archbishops, it provides fascinating background to the new rites and indicates briefly the approach to their presentation spelt out in this book. Much useful supplementary material may be found in *Prayers for Use at the Alternative Services* by Archdeacon David Silk (Mowbray).

To the acknowledgements in the first edition, I must add my indebtedness to Mrs Gina Stevens, who created an intelligible text from an almost indecipherable manuscript, and to Mr Timothy Fairbairn for reading and checking the proofs of this second edition.

Winchester 1981   MICHAEL PERHAM

1. The Priest as President

A good deal is made today of the role of the priest as an *enabler*. He is an enabler no less in the liturgy than anywhere else. He enables the people to celebrate the liturgy as worthily and helpfully as he and they are able. Every priest is different, every congregation different, every building different, and, in some sense, every Sunday of the year is different, and every Eucharist unique. No series of instructions or even guidelines can do the priest's work for him. It remains his task to develop in himself such sensitivity to the demands of the service and the needs of the people that the worship they offer to God really does touch them.

He will not achieve this without devoting time to the preparation of worship. But it will be time well spent. The public reading of the Bible needs preparation every time it is done. If they are not to be over-long and repetitious, the Intercessions need great care.

The priest will need to develop his own gestures. Those indicated in the Detailed Instructions (pp. 37ff) provide some sort of guideline. But there are no rights and wrongs in this area of worship. The priest must find a style in which he is relaxed and in which he can feel that people are being drawn together in worship. What seems appropriate to him on one occasion will suddenly seem quite inappropriate on another. The spontaneous gesture has its place in liturgy, as has the spontaneous word even within a fixed form.

The sensitive priest will also be aware of the need for variety in the way he speaks. This is not a matter of 'putting on a voice'—far from it. It is a matter of realising that some words require a dramatic declamatory voice, others a gentle, almost conversational tone. The shout and the whisper can both have their place in one service. This need for variety is particularly true of the Thanksgiving, which congregations tend to claim is too long. There is a rich variety of ideas and moods within that prayer and, if it is not to drag, these must be brought out.

None of this must be taken to mean that the priest is so to impose his personality on the celebration of the Eucharist that he becomes the focus. Too much variety, too many intrusions, can be as bad as the monotony of a Eucharist into which no apparent thought or feeling is going. So the task of the priest is not easy. He will need to listen to the comments of the people and encourage them to talk about the liturgy, including his own contribution. The priest has a special expertise in liturgy and a special role to perform, but the offering of the worship of the church is not his private domain, but the activity of the whole community in which he presides. It is that whole community that needs to be made to feel that it is celebrating the Holy Eucharist.

2. The Altar, Furnishings, and Vestments

An ideal arrangement for a celebration of the Eucharist facing the people is a slightly raised altar, close to the people, even with them on three sides of it, and chairs for the President and his assistants behind it raised slightly above it. But there will be infinite local variety dictated by considerations of size and shape. Unless the altar cannot be near the people, there is no particular virtue in conducting the first part of the service from a different part of the church. It may emphasise the distinctive elements within the service of Word and Sacrament, but in fact the Eucharist is more a symbol of their unity than their distinction. But if the altar cannot be near the people, whether because there is no room for one near them or because a nave altar would be aesthetically disastrous, it will be as well to conduct the whole of the service as far as the Peace at the chancel step. In that case no chairs are required in the sanctuary. Instead, they should be at the chancel step, facing the people, as should be a lectern in the centre. These should be sufficiently light to be removed at the Offertory if they are likely to obscure the view of the altar.

In the sanctuary, in addition to the altar, there must be a credence table. For a westward-facing celebration this ought, if possible, to be on the north (rather than the traditional south). The altar book, with cushion or stand if necessary, should lie in the centre of the altar, except from the Offertory to the

Ablutions when the elements are on the altar, during which time it is moved to the left or right. (A large stand looks very ugly and obliterates the view of the Eucharistic action at a westward-facing celebration. Better to use a cushion or just to place the book flat on the altar. The print in the altar copies of the new liturgy is very clear.) There is no need at all to remove the book from one side of the altar to the other during the service, as was the practice with the old rite at an eastward-facing celebration. The vessels, other than those that will be brought up in an offertory procession, should be placed on the credence table (not on the altar) before the service. If a ciborium is to be used, a paten is not necessary. The chalice may be covered with coloured burse and veil, but again this is quite unnecessary. On the chalice there should be purificator, corporal, and pall, brought to the altar at the Offertory (or the corporal may be placed on the altar before the service). There is a strong argument for not using any unnecessary items which clutter the altar and obscure the elements.

Presumably there will usually be lighted candles on the altar. But if there are candles carried in procession, it is appropriate if these are placed on or near the altar when the President and his assistants come to the altar, whether this is at the beginning of the service or at the Offertory.

There are several small aesthetic points which the President and his assistants will do well to note. It is a mistake ever to *kneel* behind the altar when celebrating facing the people. Any priest who does not realise this cannot ever have watched a celebration where it happens. The effect is a little ridiculous; the priest appears and disappears like a jack-in-the-box. A profound bow is a better position at such points in the service as the Confession. For the same reason, many will think it better in reverencing the elements after the Thanksgiving if those in the sanctuary bow profoundly rather than genuflect. In a somewhat similar vein, it is better for a priest celebrating behind the altar always to stand in the centre. Aesthetically this is far more pleasing than going to either end to read particular parts of the service. What looks quite natural when facing east can look very odd when facing the people.

It is an ancient and worthy custom to reverence the altar by a bow, even when there are no consecrated elements upon it. But it should be noted that it is the altar, and not the cross or crucifix, that is reverenced. Such reverence, if it is paid at all, should therefore be paid even when the cross has been removed for a westward-facing celebration. If the cross has been placed on a pedestal of some sort behind the President (a good idea if it can be done), he should of course never turn his back on the altar and reverence the cross. The reverence is shown to the altar because it is the focus of Christ's presence in the Eucharistic celebration and has itself become a sort of sacrament of Christ and his presence in the church. It is also quite wrong at a Eucharist to turn one's back on a nave altar at which the Eucharist is being celebrated to reverence a high altar in the distance. Not only the President and his assistants, but also the choir, if there is one, should bow to the altar at which the Eucharist is being celebrated, and to no other, however much more impressive another may be. It is in any case unnecessary to reverence the altar except on first entering the sanctuary and on leaving it at the end of the service. When first approaching the altar, and again when leaving it, the President and the Assistant may kiss the altar. Similarly it is quite wrong to turn to face the high altar for the *Gloria*, Creed, etc., if this means turning one's back on the altar at which the service is taking place. All should, as far as possible, face the altar or lectern (as appropriate) for the first part of the service, and the altar for the second part.

The President, if he is to wear a chasuble, should wear it throughout the service. There is no merit or point in putting it on only at the Offertory, as if what had happened up to that point was not the Eucharist. Equally pointless is the practice of wearing a cope for the first part of the service and then exchanging it for a chasuble. The habit of taking off the chasuble or cope to preach is equally strange. If the priest is to wear either of these garments (and the chasuble is certainly the more convenient in which to celebrate, as well as possessing richer historical associations) it should be worn from start to finish.

Whether the priest crosses the stole under a chasuble matters very little, but when a priest wears alb and stole without chasuble, an uncrossed stole looks better. In the Roman Church the stole is now worn uncrossed. There is nothing wrong in the stole being worn *outside* the chasuble and this can look well with the right combination of colours. In the Roman Church the wearing of the maniple has been discontinued; it is quite superfluous.

4

The Assistant will wear alb and stole. If he is a priest, he should wear the stole uncrossed; if a deacon, in the traditional way over the left shoulder.

Other assistants, or servers, may wear cassock with alb, surplice, or cotta, according to the custom of the parish. But there is also a good case for them wearing their ordinary clothes, since, like those who read or bring up the Offertory, they are doing a particular task on behalf of the people. They are not quasi-priestly figures.

3. The Preparation

[A:1–11; B:1–6; 3:1–6]

All these rites allow the service to start with a sentence, and the ASB provides such a sentence for each day. Its purpose is to set the mood or theme of the Eucharist and this should be taken up in the music of the Introit, whether the *Gloria* or *Kyries*, or a hymn, canticle or psalm.

The Greeting (A:2; B:2; 3:3) that follows is, in Rite A, mandatory and to be said by the President, however much he may delegate to others parts of the Ministry of the Word. The Greeting should be the first words addressed by the President to the people. It is peculiar to greet people when you have already said several things to them! If the priest is to explain the theme of the Eucharist, he should do it briefly after the Greeting. In Rite A the Easter alternative Greeting is always to be preferred throughout the 50 days from Easter to Pentecost. Other words of greeting are permitted. The Roman rite suggests some alternatives.

The collect for Purity (A:3; B:3; 3:4) may follow the Greeting, may be used only in the vestry, or be omitted altogether. Where the Prayers of Penitence are used at the beginning, it seems superfluous.

The *Gloria* (except in Advent and Lent) makes a very suitable processional entry. In Advent and Lent the *Kyries* can serve the same purpose. But the need to enunciate the theme of the Eucharist will usually lead to the selection of a hymn to serve as the Introit, whether as an alternative or an addition to the *Gloria* or *Kyries*. In 3 the *Kyries* and *Gloria* are alternatives and they may be treated as such in A and B. As a general, though not invariable rule, the *Gloria* is used on all Sundays of the year, outside Advent and Lent, on holy days, and daily during the periods between Christmas and Epiphany and Easter and Pentecost. At other times the *Kyries* are used, though at a weekday Eucharist it will often be unnecessary to say either. In 3 the *Kyries* have a ninefold form, in A sixfold (but permitting ninefold), in B the ninefold, sixfold or threefold. A parish will be wise to have an invariable form, whatever rite it is using.

Rite A permits the Prayers of Penitence at this point or after the Intercessions. There is a strong case in favour of this earlier position, but since all the rites permit the penitential section at the later, it is discussed in this book at section 6. The use of the penitential section at the beginning raises questions about posture. Where the penitence is later, such questions do not arise and the congregation naturally stands until the readings.

The point of the collect (A:11; B:6; 3:6) is to sum up in a short prayer the theme of the Eucharist of the day. The ASB collects are carefully chosen to fit the themes. The new *Rules to Order the Service* show that only one collect is to be said. Rule 9 states: 'On weekdays, the collect of the previous Sunday is said, unless other provision is made; on the weekdays following Christmas Day, the Epiphany, Ash Wednesday and Ascension Day, it is replaced by the collects of these Holy Days; and … on a Lesser Festival or Commemoration, it is replaced by the collect appointed for that day. The collects of Christmas Day and Easter Day are not said on Christmas Eve and Easter Eve respectively.' A second collect introduces a second theme and one that cannot be developed. Where the ASB gives two collects for one feast (e.g. Easter) a choice should be made, though the second could well be used as a Post Communion prayer.

Note 9 in Rite A indicates that 'the collect may be introduced by the words "Let us pray" and a brief bidding, after which silence may be kept'. Only the priest who is sure that his people recognise the difference between 'Let us pray' and 'Let us kneel' will risk an invitation that might result in all falling to their knees in response. The sort of 'brief bidding' intended is one like those in the Roman Missal. On the Seventh Sunday before Christmas, for instance, the priest might say:

'Let us pray for faith like our father Abraham who left his homeland trusting in God's protection.' A short silence would follow and then the collect.

4. The Ministry of the Word

[A:12–19; B:7–14; 3:7–13]

The rites all allow for three readings, the last of which must always be a Gospel reading. At the Parish Communion, two readings will often be sufficient. Whether it should be an Old Testament reading or an Epistle reading depends on the time of the year. The Old Testament lesson is mandatory on the Sundays before Christmas.

No indication is given as to who should read the lessons. Whoever does so should be chosen because of his or her ability to speak clearly and to read in a compelling way, and not because he or she holds some office in the church. There is no need for a reader to wear any special clothing to do this, and therefore the habit of assigning the readings to lay assistants at the altar is not to be commended. There is nothing to prevent a layman or laywomen from reading the Gospel. Traditionally, however, only an ordained minister reads the Gospel and, although there is no need to make this a hard and fast rule, there is some sense in having this one lesson read by a minister, and accompanied by some ceremonial, lighted candles, and perhaps a procession to the midst of the people, to mark it out as the high point of the Ministry of the Word. On the other hand, there is something to be said for all the readings coming from one place to express the unity of the Ministry of the Word. When there is a deacon present, he should read the Gospel, since this is one of the few special liturgical functions attached to his office. But there is an argument for the Gospel being read by the preacher, when there is a sermon and when it is to be in some sense an exposition of the Gospel (as it ought to be, more often than not), and the sermon preached from the same place.

Where there are three readings, a psalm is suggested by all three rites between the first two. After the second reading (or, when there are only two readings, between these) all the rites permit a canticle, a hymn, or a psalm. But the need to keep the service short will sometimes dictate that when there are three readings, two of them are read without an intervening psalm, though a short silence may be kept after any of the readings.

For a discussion of the use of psalmody, see below under *Seasonal Material*.

5. *The Intercessions*

[A:20–21; B:17–18; 3:15]

Except in churches where it is customary to stand for nearly all of the service, the Intercessions will be a part of the service for which the congregation will kneel, though there is nothing inappropriate about standing for the Intercessions.

All three rites allow for the President 'or others' to lead the Intercessions. If lay people are to do this, great care should be taken in choosing them and training them. Some have great difficulty in composing petitions that accord with the set forms (a far more difficult task than composing a prayer with no set form at all), and others cannot resist the temptation to include their favourite prayers from other services or to preach a series of mini-sermons on their pet subjects. The rubrics permit the Intercessions to be composed entirely by the reader. The set parts are not mandatory in A, where every encouragement is given to break away from set forms. In 3 the rubrics are ambiguous and have sometimes been interpreted as giving freedom to omit the set texts.

Both A and B permit alternative forms of Intercessions. In B the First Intercession is based on the 1928 Prayer. It may be said as a continuous prayer or divided into paragraphs by the versicle and response, 'Lord, in thy mercy/Hear our prayer'. Where it is so divided, paragraph 2 should be regarded as two paragraphs, the second beginning at 'Give grace, O heavenly Father . . .'. It is, presumably, only a typographical error that does not print it as such. With this form, if there are to be specific petitions, they should be brief, in no way general (for the general material is in the text) and all said before the prayer begins. This prayer does not lend itself to interpolation.

In Rite A similarly, the Litany (section 81B) must be said without interpolation, though brief biddings may be given before the Litany is begun. The other alternative form in A (81A) will not often seem adequate for a Sunday celebration, but will serve for a weekday Eucharist. Its principal deficiency is lack of commemoration of the departed, traditionally part of the Eucharistic liturgy. It is best used with the third Eucharistic Prayer (40) which compensates for that lack.

But the usual form of the Intercession will probably be that in 3, the Second Intercession in B (18) and sections 21–22 in A (though A encourages greater freedom, see below). The 3 and B form is simpler to understand, for it is divided into five very clear sections, each ending with a congregational response. A can be used in exactly the same way (regarding the last two paragraphs, both of which point to the Communion of Saints, as one section), but it is designed for greater freedom. The response may be said in each section after biddings but before the set paragraph (as in the old Series 2). The prayer may be said as a continuous whole. It is a more difficult form to use because, for instance, in the first sections additional material will need to precede the set text, whereas in the latter sections names can be inserted into the text. Making the transition from set text to extempore prayer will not always be achieved smoothly, and many people will need much guidance if they are to use this form effectively.

In some circumstances it will be possible to encourage the people to add their own petitions from the congregation, though this has its dangers and is probably not often suitable for a typical Parish Communion. Where it is not appropriate, there is much to be said for encouraging the people to write down particular intercessions and thanksgivings, leaving them at the door of the church for inclusion in the prayers the following week. In this way, if some are really not suitable in the form they are presented, small changes of emphasis can meanwhile be made by the person leading the Intercessions.

Using the B and 3 structure (which most will probably also use for A), the opening clause of each section will probably need to be quite general. But thereafter the petitions should be relatively specific, since the general is expressed quite adequately in the set parts. It is therefore unnecessary to pray for

9

the Queen (except on a special occasion like her birthday) because that will only introduce a pointless repetition. Similarly there is no need to give thanks for the lives of the saints (in A and 3), for the set part does that, though it may well be appropriate to name a particular saint on his or her day. If that is done it should be done in the fifth section, rather than the first.

The prayers are addressed to God. It is therefore quite wrong to start any clause 'Let us pray for' or, rather worse, 'Let us ask God'. In A and 3 it is always a request to 'you', in B to 'thee'. One of two styles is appropriate. Either 'We pray to you for . . .', and this is probably the easier. Or a series of imperatives, similar to those in the set parts, by which each clause is introduced by a word like 'Bless', 'Remember', 'Strengthen', 'Uphold', 'Banish', etc. The latter form is very crisp and, if well done, very effective. Any temptation to introduce other set prayers into the prayer must be resisted; the different rhythm and language makes this very unsatisfactory. Care should be taken to exclude all 'thee' forms from A and 3 and 'you' forms from B.

The use of quasi-archaic language in Rite B may provide a problem for those composing Intercessions. Quite without lawful authority, the priest may decide to use the 'you' form throughout the Intercession of B. If he does this, it really should be *throughout* and the appropriate alterations should be made to the set text as well as the variables.

In Appendix 2 (page 58) a specimen form of Intercession is given in a section which it is hoped that the parish priest may feel worth giving to members of the laity who have to lead the Intercessions.

The specimen form interprets the rubrics in a rather con-servative manner. A quite different approach is possible, and indeed greater variety is very desirable if the Intercessions are not to get 'in a rut'. Especially when very competent men and women are leading Intercessions, they can be encouraged to dispense with the set words, with the five-fold structure, even with the direct address to God (employing the bidding prayer form instead). Where the five-fold structure is abandoned, care still needs to be taken to ensure *balance* in the prayer. Where the set words are abandoned, care needs to be taken to ensure some sort of congregational response. A long solo extempore prayer will not often be the best form of the people's Intercession.

6. The Penitential Prayers

[A:4–8 or 23–29; B:19–22; 3:16–20]

Every congregation will need to decide at which point it will *normally* use the penitential material. It would be unsatisfactory for a congregation never to know the order of its service, though it would also be a pity if rigidity ruled out variety when the need occurred. The earlier position, at the beginning, makes the Confession an act of preparation for the whole service. But, theologically, the later position points to the fact that penitence, along with intercession, is a *response* to the preaching of the Gospel, expressed liturgically in the Ministry of the Word. If the penitential section is seen as *preparatory*, concerned principally with the sinfulness of the worshippers, the beginning makes better sense. If it is seen as expressing the involvement of the whole of mankind in sin, then this is much clearer in the second position.

Only Rite A allows this section at the beginning of the service, though B places the optional use of the Commandments or the Summary of the Law at the beginning. Both A and 3 wisely permit the use of these (the Commandments with New Testament comment) as an introduction to the penitential section. There are occasions in the year when these are appropriate—the First Sunday in Advent, Ash Wednesday and the First Sunday in Lent.

When the Commandments or Summary are not used, the Comfortable Words (or one or more of these) may be used to introduce the penitential section. To use both the Commandments or Summary and the Comfortable Words would obviously produce an overloading of biblical material. But, in any case, and especially when (in A) the earlier position is chosen for the penitential prayers, it is doubtful whether the Confession needs more than the briefest introduction. The second paragraph of 6 (in A), 'Let us confess our sins . . .', will usually be adequate, and even briefer forms will often serve. The priest may simply say, 'Let us confess our sins to God'. The Roman form is 'My brothers and sisters, to prepare ourselves to celebrate the sacred mysteries, let us call to mind our sins'.

The alternative Confessions in A are not sufficiently different from that in the set text to justify turning to the appendix to find variety.

Where the later position is chosen for this section, there is no difficulty about posture. The people will have been kneeling for the Intercessions and remain so until they stand for the Peace. But in Rite A, the question of posture arises if the penitential prayers are at the beginning. Many congregations will continue to find it appropriate to *kneel* for the Confession. But it would be wrong to be kneeling for the opening Greeting. The people should therefore kneel, if they are to do so, at the Invitation to Confession. But when are they to stand? Clearly the *Gloria*, as a shout of praise, should be said or sung standing. In churches where *Gloria* and *Kyries* are used as alternatives, confusion will ensue where the congregation is not sure which option is to be used. It will probably prove most satisfactory always to use the *Kyries* to conclude the penitential section and for the people always to stand immediately after it, whether the *Gloria* is to follow or the Collect without *Gloria*. The change of posture will indicate the end of the penitential section.

The prayer of Humble Access (with its alternative form in Rite A) is not mandatory in any of the rites. It is something of an intrusion between the Intercession or Absolution and the Peace. When it is used, it should be noted that Rite B places in parentheses the Prayer Book words, 'that our sinful bodies may be made clean . . .', that A and 3 omit altogether.

7. *The Peace*

[A:30–31; B:24–25; 3:21–22]

All three rites rightly instruct the people to stand for the Peace. It is not a prayer, but a declaration to the people and an exchange among them. They should therefore stand, whether or not there is to be any 'passing' of the Peace. It is quite inappropriate for the people to be kneeling, heads bowed, at this point. If they stand for the Peace, they are then in the correct position for the Offertory which follows.

When saying 'The peace of the Lord be always with you', the priest should extend his hands in a gesture of greeting to the congregation.

The passing of the Peace has engendered much controversy.

Very few people see any objection in theory to an exchange such as this as an expression of Christian fellowship. But it has been difficult in practice to devise a form that is not slightly forced or faintly ridiculous. What should the physical contact be, if there is to be any? A hug or kiss may seem out of place except in very special conditions. A formal liturgical handclasp is without parallel in daily life and therefore becomes just another rather baffling ritual. An ordinary handshake is probably best, but even this is a slightly unnatural thing, especially among the young. Certainly it is an extraordinary sight to see husband and wife solemnly shaking hands in church, because hugging or kissing in church seems to them to be stranger still. Many clergy deal with such reticence by passing the Peace only on special occasions. But this is not to be recommended. For the Peace to be anything but embarrassing and strange it needs to be so regular a part of worship that people cease to be self-conscious about it. Therefore it is probably best to press on with it at every service every week, assuring the congregation that what at first seems strange will soon cease to be.

It is unnecessary for the people to use the full form of the Peace. Turning to their neighbour, they should say 'Peace be with you, A', to which the reply should be 'And with you, B', or simply 'Peace'.

In order to avoid a situation where members of the congregation are giving the Peace only to members of their own family, they should always be encouraged to turn to greet the people in front of them and behind them.

Theologically there is something to be said for the method by which the Peace is passed from the President to his assistants and then by them to the people. But in practice this can result in a long gap before the Peace reaches some people, and this takes away all spontaneity. There is no reason why the President and his assistants should not move among the people giving the Peace, but if they do so, it should be *in addition to*, rather than *instead of*, the informal exchanges that should follow the President's greeting to the people.

8. The Preparation and Taking of the Bread and Wine

[A:32–36; B:26–28; 3:23–25]

Rite A and Series 3 avoid the use of the word 'offertory' and there has been a good deal of confusion about what symbolism is attached to this part of the service.

Rite B allows the taking and presentation of the collection ('the gifts of the People') at an earlier point. This is highly undesirable, for it separates the presentation of money from the presentation of bread and wine; and yet they both represent the work of men's hands. The Rite B rubric (15) should always be ignored. Money, bread and wine should all be brought to the altar at the 'Offertory' after the Peace. The Offertory Procession, popular in many parishes, is an appropriate symbolic action, though one not without theological difficulties. It is a pity that its use is normally restricted to the Parish Communion. Whenever there is a Eucharist at which money is brought ceremonially to the altar, bread and wine should be brought at the same time. There is no need to bless the water that is mixed with the wine.

The bread and wine should be placed on the altar by the President or his assistants without elevation or any other ceremony. All three rites provide for a sentence of praise to be said by the President and people, though Rite A indicates that this sentence is appropriate only for 'the offerings of the people' (a deliberately ambiguous phrase?). There is good liturgical argument for omitting this, for it tends to take away from the impact of the Eucharistic Prayer. What the President is doing at this point, in line with the Lord's action at the Last Supper, is not *blessing*, but *placing*. Any prayer (even said silently by the President) that is specific blessing of the elements should be avoided. But, though silence may be preferable, it does often seem natural to say something appropriate when the bread and wine are brought to the altar. The words provided are suitable and are clearly not a blessing. Those in the new Roman rite, based on Jewish prayers, are beautiful, have commended themselves to Anglican congregations and are permitted by the strange rubric in Rite A: 'The president may praise God for his gifts in appropriate words to which all respond "Blessed be God for ever"'. They read as follows:

President   Blessed are you, Lord, God of all creation. Through your goodness we have this bread to offer, which earth has given and human hands have made. It will become for us the bread of life.

People   Blessed be God for ever.

President   Blessed are you, Lord, God of all creation. Through your goodness we have this wine to offer, fruit of the vine and work of human hands. It will become our spiritual drink.

People   Blessed be God for ever.

Rite A then includes the following rubric (and 3 has similar words): 'The president takes the bread and cup into his hands and replaces them on the holy table'. The Liturgical Commission explained the rubric thus:

> This 'taking' should not be confused with the offertory and the preparation of the vessels beforehand, nor with the action that took place during the narrative of the Institution in the 1662 rite. The 'taking' is a distinct action, the first of the dominical acts made by the president, and the immediate prelude to the giving of thanks. Our Lord first 'took' bread and wine, and after this he gave thanks. In the Jewish passover meal the bread and wine were clearly on the table before they were 'taken'. The bread was lifted slightly above the table, and the cup was lifted a handsbreadth above the table; and then thanks were said over them.*

The President should do the same, not during the offertory sentence, or prayers, but as a separate action. Having 'taken' the elements, there is no need at all for him to 'take' them into his hands during the Eucharistic Prayer. But, in Rite B, the rubrics are different (see below).

If the President is to wash his hands, he should do this after the offertory sentence or prayers have been said, but before the 'taking'.

---

* *The Presentation of the Eucharist*, SPCK 1971, p. 15.

9. The Giving of Thanks

[A:37–41; B:29–32; 3:26–29]

All three rites go out of their way to show that the whole Thanksgiving is one prayer, and that to regard some part of it as specially holy is mistaken. Many churches, feeling quite rightly that the congregation is better on its feet for the praise of the *Sursum Corda* and the *Sanctus*, invite the people to kneel, just before the words of Institution. This is not a good thing and a note in Rite A discourages it: 'The Eucharistic Prayer is a single prayer, the unity of which may be obscured by changes of posture in the course of it'. Better that a congregation should kneel throughout the Thanksgiving than change half way through. But better still that they should stand throughout. For it is the ultimate prayer of praise, and standing is the traditional and natural posture for praise. If a parish wishes to retain both postures, it would be sensible to kneel for the whole prayer in Advent and Lent, but stand throughout on other Sundays of the year.

These rites, following the insights of modern liturgical thinking, avoid any idea of 'consecration' by an almost magical formula—the words of Institution. Not that the Lord's words are unimportant. They give authority to what is being done and they set it within its historical context and point to its origin. But it is through the whole Eucharistic action, of which the offering of the whole prayer is the climax, that the bread and wine are set aside to be the Body and Blood of Christ. Anything that overemphasises the words of Institution at the expense of the rest of the prayer is therefore undesirable. In particular, the ringing of bells, the elevation of the elements, and reverence paid to the elements by genuflecting or bowing after the words of Institution are best avoided.

Rite B retains the 'manual acts' (mandatory in its First Thanksgiving, optional in its Second) but simplifies them. A and 3 have no such actions during the Eucharistic Prayer—the 'taking' has already been done, the 'breaking' is following—and imply that the whole Thanksgiving is better said without the President touching or lifting the elements. Instead, the President should extend his hands throughout the prayer. A note in Rite A indicates that 'the president may use traditional manual acts during the Eucharistic Prayers'. But even if he does so, genuflections after the words of Institution should not be retained.

If the sign of the cross over the elements is thought desirable, the most suitable point is, either once or three times, at the end of the Thanksgiving at the words 'through him, and with him, and in him' or 'by whom, and with whom, and in whom'. And, if there is to be an elevation, it should be right at the end of the prayer. The First Eucharistic Prayer in Rite A builds up to a great climax and the elements may be elevated *throughout* the final acclamation.

The bread and wine should be elevated together. It is better to elevate the ciborium than simply a priest's host. If it is thought desirable to reverence the elements after the Thanksgiving, it should be done just once after the single elevation.

Great care needs to be taken with the choice of proper prefaces, especially with Rite B, since in that rite the two Eucharistic Prayers each have a different set of prefaces and the two are not interchangeable. The ASB indicates the appropriate preface, when there is one, but it remains easy for the priest to find himself using one that makes nonsense of the structure and meaning of the prayer.

10. *The Breaking of the Bread*

[A:42–44; B:33–36; 3:30–31]

Rite A reverses the Series 3 positions of the Lord's Prayer and the Fraction. Rite B prints the text of the Lord's Prayer after the Fraction, as in 3, but allows it before the Fraction, as in Rite A. For consistency's sake a parish that uses A and B will do well to adopt the Rite A order of Lord's Prayer, followed by Fraction.

In none of these rites (except the First Thanksgiving in B, and even there it is not mandatory) should the President have broken the bread during the words of Institution. As 'taking' was the first action and 'giving thanks' the second, so now 'breaking' is the third.

The Fraction raises the question of what form of bread should be used. Of course there is symbolic value in an

17

ordinary loaf of bread, but its use at the altar may not be convenient. If wafers are to be used, it is preferable to use nothing but priest's wafers, one for every four communicants. Brought to the altar in a ciborium (in which case no paten is needed at all), they can all be broken in four at the Fraction. It is possible to break a dozen of them at a time. The only argument for using the smaller traditional wafers is that they enable the congregation to put their own in the ciborium when they enter the church, a symbolic gesture with practical usefulness in assessing the number of communicants. The *Agnus Dei* (A:44; B:35; 3:34) may be said or sung at this point to cover this action if, at a very large service, it could take time to break all the wafers. But the Assistant may also break the bread with the President. Large thicker wafers, more like real bread, are now available from several suppliers. The use of these wafers is common on the continent.

The posture of the people for the Lord's Prayer and for the Fraction is not very important. But where they have been standing for the whole of the Thanksgiving, there is an argument for allowing them to kneel before the Lord's Prayer. For some the period of standing will have been long enough. On the other hand, the Roman rite orders quite the opposite. The people kneel for the Thanksgiving, but then stand for the Lord's Prayer and Fraction. And in Anglican churches where people have knelt for the Thanksgiving, to stand now may be appropriate. Variety is quite important, both for the very old and the very young.

11. The Giving of the Bread and the Cup

[A:45–49; B:37–42; 3:31–35]

The Invitation to Communion ('Draw near with faith . . .') is to be said *before* the President and his assistants receive the bread and wine. If it follows their making of Communion, it separates that action from the Communion of the people. To do so is both theologically and liturgically undesirable. The people should be encouraged to obey the instruction to 'draw near'. Immediately it has been said, the first of them should approach the altar, without waiting for any further signal. The rubrics leave it open whether the President and his assistants receive Communion before the people or after them. For them to receive last is both good manners and a fine example of what a minister should do, put himself last.

Rite A provides additional Words of Invitation in the appendix, but, strangely, insists that, at least on Sundays, and Holy Days, they be additional rather than alternative words of invitation. Their position, outside the text, will unfortunately discourage their use in many churches.

The communicant is instructed in A and 3 (in B it is optional) to reply 'Amen' to the words of administration. To allow him to do so, whoever administers the cup should allow time for this response *before* the chalice is put to the mouth. The people should be instructed to say 'Amen' at this point, and not after drinking the wine.

When, in order to avoid over-lengthy periods of inaction during the administration, there is need to employ lay men and women to help with the administration, the bishop's permission is required. It is better to have a rota of such people than only one person (lay reader or not) who always does this. If only one man does it, he becomes invested in the eyes of the congregation with a quasi-priestly status, whereas if, like the bringing of the bread and wine to the altar and the reading of lessons, this function is performed by different members of the congregation, they are seen as representative of the people. There is no need for such people to be in the sanctuary during the major part of the service. They can come to the altar just before the rest of the people and return to their places after the Communion. But it is distressing for people to receive Communion from those who administer the chalice clumsily, and therefore this task should not be undertaken, except in emergency, without careful practice.

The President and his assistants should receive Communion standing around the altar and passing the elements one to another. With the bread, they should all take the bread into their hands; the President then says the words of administration, the assistants reply, and all together eat the bread. With the cup, each has to receive separately, but the words of administration and the reply can be said together first.

In some congregations the people will wish to receive

standing, though few churches have yet tried this, feeling no doubt that there is little virtue in forcing this against the devotional habits of a lifetime. Communion need not of course be given at a rail; people can come to ministers who remain stationary to administer. Though on very large occasions such arrangements would speed up the administration considerably, they are not worth it if they disturb the people sufficiently that their Communion is spoilt for them. The pastoral need must prevail; but such arrangements in the Roman Church do not seem to have caused great dismay.

The unconfirmed should be made welcome at the altar rail and blessed by whoever administers the bread. It should be the *unconfirmed*, and not simply *children*, who should be invited to the altar. There are present at Parish Communions today an increasing number of unconfirmed adults. The task of those administering is made far easier if those who are unconfirmed are asked to bring a prayer book with them to the altar and hold it in their hands, so that it can be seen immediately who is unconfirmed, or else they must be instructed to keep their heads bowed. This is specially important when a new or visiting clergyman is taking part in the administration. In blessing the unconfirmed, the priest should say something like 'May Almighty God bless you', adding the name of the person if he knows it. He may make the sign of the cross or, rather better, especially with children, place his hand on their heads, since the touch will mean more to a child than the words.

The three rites all permit the singing of hymns and anthems during the administration. Series 3 allows the singing of the *Benedictus*, *Agnus Dei* and other hymns during 'The Communion'. It has already been indicated by a heading that by 'The Communion' is meant the whole of the service from the Peace onwards. The *Benedictus* may therefore be sung in the traditional place after the *Sanctus*, though its presence there is not necessary. The *Agnus Dei* may be sung after the Fraction, but again this is unnecessary unless there are a great many wafers to be broken. Normally, if sung at all, these anthems will best be sung during the Communion of the people. The habit of singing a succession of eucharistic hymns during the Communion of the people, as if no silence could possibly be allowed, is undesirable. But to sing just one is reasonable. If the choir is to sing an anthem, this is the point to do so,

20

providing that it is suitable to this point in the service. If it is
not, a better place may well be between two of the readings in
the Ministry of the Word.

12. After Communion

[A:50–56; B:43–51; 3:36–45]

All three rites provide for a post-communion sentence reflecting the theme or season. If this is used, it should precede,
rather than follow, any period of silence and provide an idea
for thought and prayer during the silence. This may be the
point for the Ablutions, but if the altar is close to the people
this action will disturb the silence. The Ablutions can be done
before the sentence, in which case the President now takes his
part in the collective silence, and this is far better than
conveying the impression that the silence is simply a gap while
he is performing more actions. Alternatively, the Ablutions can
wait at a sung service until the final hymn.

A and B both indicate that the final hymn should be sung
before the Prayers, Blessing and Dismissal, whereas 3 places it
after the Prayers before the Blessing. During the hymn the
Ablutions may be done, and the President and his assistants
may go to a point closer to the people, perhaps the chancel
step, for the concluding part of the rite that follows.

It is inappropriate for the Ablutions to be done at the altar,
and it is unsightly at a westward-facing celebration. Before the
President (and the Assistant) have consumed what remains of
the consecrated elements, the vessels should be taken to the
credence table (or in a large church at a service with a big
congregation to the altar of a nearby side chapel). There is no
need to use wine in the Ablutions. Water is quite sufficient. Nor
is there any need to cover the vessels, now that they are not to
be used again.

All three rites provide (a) a long prayer to be said by the
President and (b) a short prayer for all to say together. In all

21

three cases, both prayers may be used, but they are often better regarded as *alternatives*. In Rite A the rubric allows for other suitable prayers. Where the ASB provides more than one collect for a particular day, one can be used as a post-communion, but there remains a need for the composition of seasonal post-communion prayers. David Silk provides some in *Prayers for Use at the Alternative Services* and the Scottish Prayer Book makes some provision.

Rite B and 3 permit the *Gloria* at this point (3 as a 'canticle'), though the earlier point at the beginning of the service is preferable. Rite B allows a hymn here, in addition or instead of one after Communion. But Rite A is clear that the Blessing and Dismissal should follow immediately.

All three rites provide a series of seasonal Blessings. There is no particular reason why people should kneel for the Prayers and Blessing. They have been standing for the hymn. If they remain standing for the Prayers, Blessing and Dismissal, they are in the right posture for the departure of the President and his assistants and, if there is one, the choir. If there are any last minute notices to be given by the President, he should do this *before* the final Dismissal (and before the Blessing if it is given). All three rites indicate that the President dismisses the people. Traditionally this has been the task of the Deacon. There should be no further hymn or prayers after the Dismissal. Even vestry prayers seem a little superfluous.

13. Seasonal Material

The publication of the ASB, with its adequate provision of sentences, prefaces and other variable material, will greatly enrich the celebration of the varying feasts and seasons of the Church's year. Those who use Series 3 will do well to supplement that rite's seasonal material with the new provisions of the ASB.

The Rules to Order the Service proposed in 1978, and included in the ASB, allow for one collect only to be said at the Eucharist. Certainly there is no need whatever to add the collect of the Sunday when a saint's day, even a 'black-letter' day, is being observed. The collect gives the theme of the service. To use more than one collect is to introduce a second theme which cannot be taken up in the readings and other variable material.

The ASB indicates for both Rite A and Rite B what Proper prefaces are to be used, though the provision for some days is mandatory and for others optional. The 1978 proposed rules govern the provision for Series 3:

> The Proper Thanksgiving of Advent is said from Advent Sunday until Christmas Day; of Christmas, until the Epiphany; of the Epiphany, until the Ninth Sunday before Easter; of Lent, from Ash Wednesday until Palm Sunday; of Passiontide, on Palm Sunday and the six days following; of Easter, until Ascension Day; of Ascension Day, until Pentecost; of Pentecost, for six days after: except that they are replaced by the Proper Thanksgiving of Maundy Thursday, The Presentation of Christ in the Temple, The Annunciation, the Festivals of Saints, and The Dedication of a Church, on their appointed days. (Note: in this Rule the word 'until' is used exclusively.)

Provision is made in all the rites for a psalm, or part of a psalm, to be said or sung at the Introit and during the Ministry of the Word. But there is nothing to suggest that this rubric is intended to cover only sung services; and at a said service psalms may well be said at these points. It seems unnecessary to have both a seasonal sentence and a psalm at the Introit, but a psalm between the readings fits well. The ASB provides psalms as part of the propers for every occasion and in most editions includes *The Liturgical Psalter*, also available independently from Collins. *The Psalms: A New Translation*, issued by The Grail and published by Fontana, is not authorised, but its language accords with that of Rite A and Series 3. The Revised Psalter is suitable with Rite B, but its archaic language makes it unsuitable for use with the modern language rites.

Where congregational copies are not available, the method employed in the new Roman Missal (which uses the Grail translation) has much to commend it. The President reads the verses of the psalms and the people reply at the end of each verse with a response which can be memorised or, rather better, typed on to the weekly duplicated sheet of notices, if the parish has one. The psalm appointed in the ASB for Easter Day, set out as a responsorial psalm in the Grail translation, reads like this:

All	This day was made by the Lord; we rejoice and are glad.
President	The Lord is my strength and my song; he was my saviour. There are shouts of joy and victory in the tents of the just.
All	This day was made by the Lord; we rejoice and are glad.
President	The Lord's right hand has triumphed; his right hand raised me up. The Lord's right hand has triumphed; I shall not die, I shall live and recount his deeds. I was punished, I was punished by the Lord, but not doomed to die.
All	This day was made by the Lord; we rejoice and are glad.
President	Open to me the gates of holiness: I will enter and give thanks. This is the Lord's own gate where the just may enter. I will thank you for you have given answer and you are my saviour.
All	This day was made by the Lord; we rejoice and are glad.
President	The stone which the builders rejected has become the corner stone. This is the work of the Lord, a marvel in our eyes.
All	This day was made by the Lord; we rejoice and are glad.

(Psalm 118. 4–24)

A selection of responsorial psalms is provided in *English Praise*, the supplement to the *English Hymnal*. *A Responsorial Psalm Book*, edited by Geoffrey Boulton Smith and published by Collins, gives responsorial psalms following the Roman propers for the year. It includes a variety of approaches to psalmody, some more successful than others. The whole question of psalms for singing in worship today is examined in *The Psalms: Their Use and their Performance Today*, published by the Royal School of Church Music and obtainable from The Publications Department, Addington Palace, Croydon, (price £1·25 net).

14. The Use of Silence

Silence is permitted in these rites after the Readings, Sermon, Eucharistic Prayer and Communion, during the Intercessions and before the Confession. There is something to be said for silence at all these points in the service. But clearly in one service to observe a silence at every one of them would be inappropriate. Too long a silence can in any case destroy a gathering momentum the service may have as it builds to its climax. For this reason the very best time for silence is after the climax has been reached, i.e. after Communion, though short silences during the Intercessions and before the Confession are obviously appropriate. Whenever possible the President and his assistants should take part in the corporate silence. In other words, the silence should not be simply to cover their activity. In order that the congregation can make the best use of silence, the priest will be well advised, at first at least, to say, 'Let us keep a time of silence', else half the congregation will simply spend the silence wondering what has gone wrong. Similarly he will be advised to tell the congregation how long the silence is to last and to keep to that length of time regularly, else they will spend their time wondering how much longer it will go on. If they know that week after week they have a certain precise length of time, they will learn to use that time constructively. If they never know how long it will be, they will never be able to learn to use it.

15. Concelebration

The practice of concelebration has grown considerably in recent years. When there is a concelebration, there is nevertheless always a Eucharistic President. The role of the concelebrating clergy is to share between them some of the readings, prayers, and functions of the Assistant, and to join in the saying of the Thanksgiving. But the Greeting, the Collect, the Absolution, the Peace, the opening responsory of the Thanksgiving, the Breaking of Bread and the Blessing should always be said by the President alone.

Concelebration is particularly appropriate when the President is the Bishop. It symbolises the unity of his ministry with that of the parochial clergy. There are other occasions, such as Maundy Thursday, when the clergy will wish to share in the great celebration of the day. There is much to be said for a Religious Community, or a Dean and Chapter, or a Rector and his Team Vicars, concelebrating. It gives the priests the opportunity to exercise their specific priestly role in the Eucharist. It is also a good thing for a congregation to *see*. A choir sings together, a college of priests celebrates together. But there are disadvantages in concelebration. One is a theological difficulty. It is doubtful whether a congregation celebrating a Eucharist with its President has much need of a host of 'Vice-presidents' trying to share the President's role. If all participants in the Eucharist are indeed its celebrants, what is it that these additional priestly celebrants contribute? Another disadvantage is that the Thanksgiving, if said by a number of voices together, can lack the dramatic clear-cut tone that is needed. The Concelebrants should say the Thanksgiving *quietly*, while the President speaks in a loud, clear voice and sets the pace. Or else they may stand silently. Concelebration need not mean the recitation of words.

When the Bishop comes, he should always be the President of the Eucharist, whether it is a concelebration or not. The traditional idea that he 'presided' while another priest 'celebrated' makes nonsense of any intelligent theology of episcopacy and ministry.

The Concelebrants should all wear either alb, stole, and chasuble, or else simply alb and uncrossed stole, while the

President alone wears the chasuble (and, if a bishop, the mitre).

The position in the chancel and sanctuary of the Concelebrants will depend on the space available. If they first approach the altar when the President does so, and if he kisses the altar, they do so too. Ideally they should be grouped around the President in a semi-circle throughout the service. But in some churches it will be necessary for all but the one who acts as Assistant to sit in choir until the Peace. They should certainly be grouped around the President for the Peace and all that follows.

In the Thanksgiving, whatever is sung the President sings alone; whatever is said, the Concelebrants say with him. Throughout the Thanksgiving they stand around the altar with hands extended until the elevation, when as many of them as are needed join in elevating the elements. When the President bows or genuflects after the Thanksgiving, they bow profoundly. At a large service several of them may help with the Fraction, the administration of Communion, and the Ablutions. They themselves receive Communion together standing around the altar.

16. The Daily Eucharist

The recommendations in this booklet are designed to meet the needs of the main Sunday Eucharist. Clearly the requirements for a weekday service in a parish with a daily or almost daily Eucharist will be different. Quite what those differences will be depends on the congregation at the Eucharist. In some churches the weekday service is something for the team of clergy and it is unrealistic to expect the laity to be present. In others there is a single priest who gathers around him a small devout congregation of laity.

The priest has the option of combining the morning (or sometimes the evening) office with the Eucharist. How he is to do this is indicated on page 71 of the ASB. The advantage of this is that the morning (or evening) worship has shape and balance. Without it the total Ministry of the Word can become a very long exercise with up to five lessons. But there are disadvantages. The office is a form of worship that has a rhythm of its own that includes no really high points. The Eucharist, however, is a form of worship that builds up to climaxes even in the Ministry of the Word where the gospel becomes just such a climax. The Eucharist can therefore lose something if, in accordance with the rubrics, the Ministry of the Word is replaced by Morning or Evening Prayer.

Some clergy will prefer the Eucharistic shape but use material from the office within it. The office/Ministry of the Word would then begin like this:

1 Canticle (one of those appointed for the office)
2 Greeting
3 Penitential Prayers
4 *Gloria* (optional)
5 Collect of the Day
6 Lesson (The OT lesson appointed for the office)
7 Psalm (The psalm appointed for the office)
8 Gospel (The NT lesson appointed for the office).

The Morning or Evening collect could be used as the variable post-communion prayer. This is better but a serious disadvantage remains. The Eucharist is at its best with a thematic approach—the ASB propers have shown up the Prayer Book's somewhat haphazard approach for the confusion it was. But the combining of office and Eucharist in this way would mean introducing into the Eucharist large chunks of psalmody and Scripture chosen without any reference to theme, or, most of the time, to the season of the year.

The priest may therefore prefer to keep the office and Eucharist separate. What then is he to read for the lessons at the Eucharist if he is not simply to repeat day after day the Sunday lections? Lack of weekday provision has led in the past to overburdening the calendar with a vast number of saints and *votives* to avoid monotony. One solution lies in the use of the weekday lections of the Roman Church, a carefully devised scheme with a good deal to commend it, but with the disadvantage that it has no bearing on the Series 3 themes.

It is this Lectionary that is found, with little adaptation, in Table 4 on page 1071 of the ASB. But it is a pity that the book does not contain a genuinely Anglican weekday lectionary reflecting the Anglican calendar and themes. Carefully used, the

ASB's own lections can provide a good deal of variety. Assuming that a weekday Eucharist usually has only two readings, and making use of both the Year 1 and Year 2 readings and the rather richer variety of readings for saints' days and special intentions, the priest can avoid much repetition. What repetition there is, is just enough to underline and strengthen the theme of the week.

At the daily Eucharist some variety of approach to the Intercessions will be needed. The priest may dispense entirely with the set form. Or he may make a number of biddings and then read the set prayer as a continuous whole. Or, if he does use the prayer in its five sections, he will be advised to include in each section only one or two very specific petitions, else he will find himself developing a very set and invariable form of Intercessions in which there is little spontaneity and freshness.

Some thought must be given to the posture of the people at a weekday Eucharist. In many churches where this has been thought through in relation to the Sunday Eucharist, on a weekday the people still kneel, save for the readings and Creed, throughout the Eucharist. Yet kneeling is quite inappropriate for some parts of the service, notably the Peace. Quite apart from that, the small weekday Eucharist provides an excellent opportunity to gather around the Lord's table in a literal way that is not often possible on a Sunday. Before the Offertory the people can come up into the sanctuary and stand around the altar until after the Communion.

17. Sung or Said

The parish priest has to make his own judgement on how much of the service is to be sung. The tradition of his church, the competence of the choir, and his own ability to sing will all need to be taken into account. A priest who cannot sing competently should avoid singing as much as possible. Some parts of the service he can say rather than sing, other parts can be sung for him by a cantor, probably a member of the choir.

The chanting of readings is not normally to be encouraged. The dramatic and sensitive reading of the Scriptures, with great care for variety and right emphasis, will make far more impact than a form of proclamation that plays down subtleties of meaning and takes out the dramatic. When the Gospel is said, it is better that the announcement of it and the acclamations at the beginning and end of it should also be said. In A and 3 especially, the wording of the Gospel acclamations seem to call for a *shout*, rather than for singing.

The collect introduces and sets the theme for the readings that follow it. Though it may be sung, it will appear more obviously related to the readings if it is said.

Those who have composed music for the new translation have not usually provided music for the Creed. Quite rightly it has been felt that the Creed, which is not a hymn of praise but a statement of belief, is better said. Against this there is a view that, when it is said, the period of time without singing, right from the Gradual Hymn to the Offertory, through Gospel, Sermon, Creed and Prayers, is very long. To meet this need a rubric in 3 (at section 14) and B (at section 15), but not in A, permits the singing of a hymn after the Creed.

The first part of the Eucharistic Prayer may be sung. The music provided for the President in the altar edition of the ASB is an adaption of the traditional music and is suitable for use with most settings, though many, of course, have their own setting of the *Sursum Corda*. The President's music in the altar edition of 3 is written for the Dearnley/Wicks setting and does not adapt to other settings. Unlike the Prayer Book preface, the preface in the new rites is very long and the argument against such a prolonged piece of solo singing, except by an exceptional singer, is strong.

If the President is to say, rather than sing, the first part of the Thanksgiving, it is probably better if the opening responses of it are also said. The *Sanctus* will usually be sung and, in all three rites, *Benedictus* may follow immediately. At the end of the Thanksgiving in 3, and the First Eucharistic Prayer in A, the acclamation, *Blessing and honour* . . ., can either be shouted or sung. In Rite B the *Benedictus* can be used at that later point to meet the same need as the climax of the prayer. In A and 3 the earlier set of acclamations, *Christ has died* . . ., lend themselves to a dramatic spoken response almost of a shout. In order not to mix styles too much, the priest will probably find it best to opt for one or the other, sung or dramatically spoken, for the congregational parts of the Thanksgiving. *Sursum Corda, Sanctus* and acclamations can all be sung or all said. A mixture, whereby some are sung and some not, is probably not a happy compromise.

The training of the people to speak their parts of the liturgy with sensitivity to what the particular words demand is a difficult but important part of the priest's work. Where he has a choir, it should be able to give the lead that is required. If the liturgy of the parish is really to come alive, he must somehow impress upon his choirmaster and choir that the leading of the spoken words of the liturgy is a vital part of their work. Especially in A and 3, the clear crisp enunciation of such phrases as 'Praise to Christ our Lord' and 'Christ has died' will make all the difference. The congregation will no doubt follow a good choir, but the priest should not hesitate to spend some time in developing this sort of response in the congregation.

The whole question of music for the new rites is examined more thoroughly in *Music and the Alternative Service Book*, published by the Addington Press, and edited by Lionel Dakers.

18. Liturgical Colours

In the Church of England no liturgical colour is ever ordered. The priest is free to use the colour or colours he thinks appropriate to a particular occasion. He should exercise that freedom and not feel bound to follow a convention when a particular mood or occasion seems to demand something else. The ideas here are no more than a general indication of what is appropriate. Every church seems to have a different collection and combination of colours, and so local variety will in any case be necessary.

Liturgical revision envisages a very simple calendar of the year. There are two great festival seasons, each beginning and ending with a great feast. The first begins on Christmas Day and ends on the Feast of Epiphany. The second begins on Easter Day and ends on the Feast of Pentecost. Both festival periods are preceded by solemn periods of preparation,

Advent and Lent. *White* is the colour of the festival seasons, *purple* of the periods of preparation, *green* of the rest of the year. There are other occasions on which particular colours are appropriate.

White is used for the great festival periods, on the Conversion of St Paul, the Presentation of Our Lord in the Temple, Trinity Sunday, the Birth of St John the Baptist, the Transfiguration of Our Lord, St Michael and All Angels, All Saints' Day, St John the Evangelist, feast days of the Blessed Virgin Mary and of those saints not venerated as martyrs, the Feast of Dedication of the church, at the Eucharist of the Last Supper on Maundy Thursday (and at *Corpus Christi* where this is kept) and at Baptisms, Marriages, Funerals, and Requiems.

Red is used on the Feast of Pentecost,* during Holy Week (except at the Eucharist of the Last Supper on Maundy Thursday), in honour of the Holy Spirit and of martyrs. Red or white is used at Confirmations.

Purple is used during Advent and from Ash Wednesday until the day before Palm Sunday (except where there is Lenten Array). It may be used for Funerals and Requiems, as may *Black*, but white is to be preferred.

Green is used on all days outside the two great festival periods and periods of preparation before them, except where other provision is made.

The principal changes from the traditional usage are that purple is not used on the three Sundays before Lent, on the Rogation Days, Ember Days, vigils, or (usually) at Funerals and Requiems. On Ember Days, Rogation Days and at Eucharists for special intentions such as unity, peace, etc., the colour of the Sunday is used.

The colour for a particular service should reflect the theme. If, on a saint's day, the collect, readings, etc., are of the saint, then red or white is used. If the saint is merely commemorated with an additional collect and the theme is that of the Sunday (but against this practice see page 6), the colour of the Sunday is retained.

* The new calendar does not envisage the observance of *octaves*. These are superseded by the festival periods culminating in a feast. But one week of the year proves a problem. At present, though Eastertide reaches its climax and end on the Feast of Pentecost, a further week of celebration is ordered. While this is so, red must be the colour for the whole of Whitweek, even though it would be logical to go into green as soon as the Great Fifty Days were over.

The colours indicated in the ASB accord with these principles (except for the illogical use of white on the First Sunday after Epiphany, as if the feast had an octave or, more precisely, part of one). The ASB colours are in any case optional.

19. The Use of Incense

There are no rules in the Church of England governing the use of incense, and so, in the parish where its use is appropriate, there is freedom to use it as the parish priest thinks best. No reference is made to the use of incense in the Detailed Instructions on pages 37ff, but only small modifications need be made to include an extra server to carry the censer or thurible.

If incense is to be used, it may either burn throughout the service or else be used at certain points to high-light their importance. It may simply be allowed to burn or it may be used to indicate the holiness or purifying of particular objects. If it is simply to be left to burn in the sanctuary throughout the service, then it is brought in already alight as part of the procession at the beginning and hung in the sanctuary. It will no doubt need attention at points in the service and at the end it is either carried out or may be left until after the service if the exit of the clergy is a short abrupt unceremonial one.

Even when it is not simply being left to burn, but is being used at particular points in the service, it is undesirable that there should be unnecessary processions in and out of the vestry. Such processions detract from the central action of the liturgy.

It is appropriate to cense the altar, but once in the service is quite sufficient. The time to do this is at the Offertory when the elements have already been placed upon it and may be censed at the same time.

The diagram below indicates how the priest may cense a free-standing altar. He first censes the elements, then the cross if there is one, then as indicated.

The reader of the Gospel may cense the book after announc-

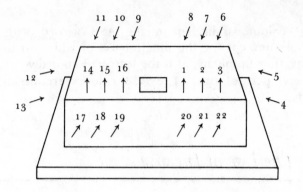

ing the Gospel and before reading it, but the symbolism here is not so appropriate. Nor is it particularly appropriate to cense people. But if the priest and people are to be censed, they should all be, without distinction. Censing separately a variety of clergymen present in order of rank and seniority is totally inappropriate. All belong equally together in the celebration of the Eucharist.

When the President (or Assistant) places incense on the charcoal, the President may make the sign of the cross in blessing over it. At a concelebration the Concelebrant who places the incense on the charcoal blesses it himself.

20. The Ministers

The President, or chief Celebrant, is the only minister necessary to every Eucharist. At a said Eucharist, or 'plain celebration', he may be assisted by one other priest or deacon called the Assistant who may also act as a server, or else by a server (who is not a clergyman) who does not therefore perform the functions of the Assistant, but may read lessons or lead intercessions. Or the President may have no other person with him in the sanctuary, but a member of the congregation may come up to the altar to assist him at the Offertory and Ablutions, and may read lessons or lead intercessions from his or her place in the congregation.

The Assistant, whether priest or deacon, stands on the President's right at the Eucharist and may perform certain functions which, if there is no Assistant, the President himself performs.

At a sung Eucharist, or 'solemn celebration', there may also be two servers or acolytes. If there are only two servers available, it is preferable to have them as acolytes, carrying lighted candles, than to employ them as a crucifer, 'master of ceremonies', etc. Indeed, if there is an Assistant, there is no need at all for a 'master of ceremonies'. Only one function is not easily performed by the Assistant or the acolytes. This is the carrying and holding of the Gospel book. Two solutions present themselves. The first is that the crucifer, if there is one and if he is no longer holding the cross, can do this. Or, if there is no crucifer or he is still occupied, the Gospel can perhaps be read from the pulpit or lectern, in which case the Assistant himself carries the Gospel book there, and it is not necessary for any-one to hold it during the reading.

If the whole service is conducted from the altar, then the crucifer, if there is one, carries the cross in procession at the beginning and end of the service, but at no other time. If the first part of the service is taken from the chancel step, he may stand with the cross, facing the people, behind the President for the first part of the service. In very few churches (except where incense is used or very elaborate ceremony employed) will it be necessary to have more than three servers—two acolytes and a crucifer. In a church where lighted candles are not carried, two servers nevertheless accompany the President and do all that the following order suggests that the acolytes do, except carry the candles.

Where the word 'assistants' is used in the plural in this booklet, it refers to all who are in the sanctuary with the President; this has sometimes been called 'the altar party'.

When in the sanctuary the President and his assistants will normally be standing in these positions:

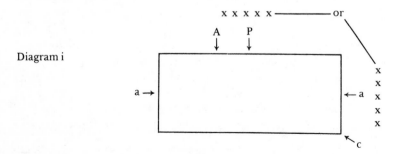

Diagram i

35

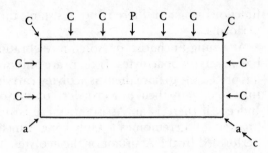

Diagram ii
At a concelebration

If the first part of the Eucharist is at the chancel step, the arrangement would be as close as possible to this:

Diagram iii

```
              c
              ↓
           x x x
   x  a →  A  P  ← a  x
           ↓  ↓
           ☐ lectern
```

Abbreviations:

P President
A Assistant
C Concelebrants
a acolytes
c crucifer
x chairs for President and assistants

Appendix 1—Detailed Instructions

Every church will need to work out for itself the detail of its ceremonial, depending very much both on space available in the church and also on personnel. The suggestions set out below assume a sung Eucharist at a free-standing altar, with the whole service taking place at it (but with some indication of variations if there is an altar at the east end and the first part of the service is at the altar step), a celebration facing the people, with two clergymen (one the President, the other the Assistant, whether priest or deacon) and three servers, two being acolytes, the third performing several functions including that of crucifer. These suggestions should not be followed slavishly but adapted to local needs. Where in the earlier pages of the booklet alternative ways of doing things have been indicated, only one is selected here, often the least traditional way, but there is nothing to prevent the reintroduction of some gestures and ritual acts that are not indicated, provided that they are consonant with the theology of the rite. The suggested order is set out in four columns. In the first is given the partial text of Rite A (nearly all the rubrics and some of the actual words of the liturgy). The second column gives notes on the functions of the President and the Assistant, the third the functions of the servers, at each point in the service. The fourth column includes various notes, a good many of which relate to the adaptation that is needed if B or 3 is used.

Holy Communion Rite A

The Preparation

The Assistant may read notices and banns before the service and he may announce the hymn, returning to the vestry to join in the procession.

1 At the entry of the ministers AN APPROPRIATE SENTENCE may be used; and A HYMN, A CANTICLE, or A PSALM may be sung.

After bowing to the altar (and kissing it, if they so wish), the President and the Assistant take up their positions behind the altar facing the people, the Assistant on the President's right.

2 The president welcomes the people using these or other appropriate words
    The Lord be with you
All **and also with you.**
or
    The Lord is here.
All **His Spirit is with us.**
or Easter Day to Pentecost
    Alleluia! Christ is risen.
All **He is risen indeed. Alleluia!**

The President says this, with hands extended.

Prayers of Penitence
4 THE PRAYERS OF PENITENCE (sections 5–8) may be said here, or after section 23; if they are said here, sections 6–8 are always used. Alternative confessions may be used (see section 80).

5 THE COMMANDMENTS (section 78) or the following SUMMARY OF THE LAW may be said:
Minister Our Lord Jesus Christ . . .

If this section is used, Advent Sunday, Ash Wednesday and Lent 1 are suitable days. The Assistant may read this section.

38

The choir may enter before these notices if it is not to form part of the procession.

It is unnecessary to use a sentence if there is a hymn. The hymn should set the theme of the Eucharist.

Order of procession: (1) Crucifer and Acolytes; ((2) Choir;) (3) Assistant; (4) President.

After bowing to the altar, the acolytes take up the position indicated in diagram i (p. 35). The candles are placed on or near the altar. The crucifer puts the cross wherever it is to remain during the service and takes up the position indicated in the diagram.

For notes on psalmody, see page 23. But if the first part of the service is at the chancel step, the President and his assistants take up the positions indicated in diagram iii (p. 36) and the crucifer continues to hold the cross and the acolytes their candles.

Using Series 3, turn now to the *Kyries*.

Holy Communion Rite A

6 The minister invites the congregation to confess their sins in these or other suitable words (see section 25).
God so loved the world . . .

The Assistant may say this.

7 All **Almighty God, our heavenly Father . . .**

The Assistant may begin the Confession. The President and Assistant say the Confession standing, but with heads bowed.

8 President Almighty God,
who forgives all . . .

The President makes the sign of the cross at 'pardon and deliver you' when saying the Absolution.

9 KYRIE ELEISON may be said (see also section 79).

10 GLORIA IN EXCELSIS may be said.

The President need not sing the opening words of the *Gloria* alone.

11 The president says THE COLLECT.

The President reads this with hands extended.

The Ministry of the Word

12 Either two or three readings from scripture follow, the last of which is always the Gospel.

13 Sit

The President and the Assistant sit.

OLD TESTAMENT READING
At the end the reader may say
This is the word of the Lord.
All **Thanks be to God.**

40

Using Rite B, turn now to the *Kyries* or *Gloria*. Section 25 contains 'The Comfortable Words'.

The servers say the Confession standing but with heads bowed.

The people kneel. Silence may be kept before the Confession.

A threefold, sixfold or ninefold form may be used. In 3 the *Kyries* and *Gloria* are alternatives, possibly the *Kyries* in Advent and Lent. They may be treated as such in B, but in A it is preferable always to say the *Kyries* (see page 12).

The people stand even if, on weekdays that are not holy days, or on Sundays in Advent and Lent, *Gloria* is not to be sung.

In the Roman rite, the sign of the cross is no longer made at the end of the *Gloria*.

The crucifer brings the book in which the collect is written and stands with it before the President only if there is no altar (or lectern) on which the book can have been placed.

The servers sit.

But if at the chancel step (as in diagram iii) the crucifer continues to stand until after the gospel.

This may be omitted if 15 is read. If it is read, a member of the congregation reads it. Silence may be kept after the reading.

14 A PSALM may be used.

The President and the Assistant may stand, unless the choir sings alone, in which case they may remain seated. The psalm may be announced by the Assistant.

15 NEW TESTAMENT READING (EPISTLE)
At the end the reader may say
    This is the word of the Lord.
All **Thanks be to God.**

The President and the Assistant sit.

16 A CANTICLE, A HYMN, or A PSALM may be used.

The President and the Assistant may stand, unless the choir sings alone, in which case they remain seated. The 'gradual' may be announced by the Assistant.

During the gradual, the Assistant (unless he is a Concelebrant) may bow before the President who says: 'The Lord be in your heart and on your lips: that you may worthily and joyfully proclaim his holy gospel: In the Name of the Father, and of the Son ✣ and of the Holy Spirit. Amen.' or similar words.

If the Gospel is to be read from the nave, the Assistant takes the Gospel book from the altar (before being blessed by the President). He carries it to the place where the Gospel is to be read. (But see page 7.) If the President is to preach the Sermon, he may follow the Gospel procession and go to the pulpit now.

17 Stand

THE GOSPEL. When it is announced
All **Glory to Christ our Saviour.**
At the end the reader says
    This is the Gospel of Christ.
All **Praise to Christ our Lord.**

The Assistant reads the Gospel. If he is speaking for the first time to the people he may greet them first. The President stands and faces the Gospel procession.

Servers	*Notes*

The servers stand if the President does so.

This may be omitted. For notes on psalmody see page 23. The people stand if the President does so.

The servers sit.

This may be omitted if 13 is read. If it is read, a member of the congregation reads it. Silence may be kept after the reading.

The servers stand if the President does so.

The people stand if the President does so.

This may be the best point for the choir to sing an anthem.

The acolytes with candles precede the Assistant. The crucifer (without cross) follows them if he is to hold the Gospel book during the Gospel. Or if the crucifer is not required to hold the book, he may lead the procession with the cross.

A Gospel procession would seem unnecessary if the Ministry of the Word is at the chancel step.

For further notes on the Gospel procession and Reading, see page 7.

The people stand, if they are not already doing so, and face the Gospel reader.

In the Roman rite the Gospel reader makes the sign of the cross on the book; on his forehead, mouth and breast. The custom of facing north for the Gospel has no modern point.

Silence may be kept after the Gospel.

Holy Communion Rite A

At the end of the Gospel, the Assistant may kiss the book.

The Assistant returns to his seat (unless he is to preach in which case he goes to the pulpit).

18 Sit
THE SERMON

The preacher returns to his seat. If there is a silence he sits.

19 Stand
THE NICENE CREED is said on Sundays and other Holy Days, and may be said on other days.

The President and Assistant stand.
If the Creed is sung, the President need not sing the opening words alone.

The Intercession

20 INTERCESSIONS AND THANKS-GIVINGS are led by the president, or by others. The form below, or one of those in section 81, or other suitable words, may be used.

Before the Intercession the President says 'Let us kneel to pray', unless the people are to remain standing for the Intercession.

(23 THE PRAYERS OF PENITENCE (sections 24–28) are said here, if they have not been said after section 4.)

29 All may say
We do not presume . . .
The alternative prayer at 82 may be used.

The Ministry of the Sacrament

The Peace

30 Stand
The president says either of the following or other suitable words (see section 83).

The President may need to invite the people to stand at the beginning of this section.

Servers	_Notes_
The servers precede the Assistant and return to their seats.	If the Ministry of the Word has been at the chancel step, at this point the crucifer, who has been holding the cross throughout, puts it aside and sits.
	All sit.
	Silence may be kept after the Sermon.
The servers stand when the President does so. They return to their positions and face the altar rather than the east.	The people stand when the President does so. All may bow at the name of Jesus and at 'By the power of the Holy Spirit he became incarnate of the Virgin Mary, and was made man'.
	In the Roman rite the sign of the cross is no longer made at the end of the Creed.
The servers do not kneel.	See page 8 and Appendix 2 for detailed discussion of the Intercession.
	This order assumes that the Prayers of Penitence have been said at the earlier point (see pages 38–41). In Rite B and 3 they must be used at this point, but the notes on pages 38–41 apply.
	This may be omitted.

Christ is our peace . . .
or We are the Body of Christ . . .
He then says
  The peace of the Lord be
  always with you
All **and also with you.**

The President should say this with hands extended. If the Peace is to be exchanged, he may greet all the assistants. Even if there is no general exchange of the Peace he may give it to the Assistant.

31 The president may say
  Let us offer one another a sign
  of peace.
 and all may exchange a sign of
 peace.

The Preparation of the Gifts

The Assistant may announce the Offertory hymn.

32 The bread and wine are placed on
  the holy table.

The Assistant receives the gifts. The Offertory procession comes to the altar.

The Assistant lays the collection on the altar, without blessing it or raising it.

The Assistant lays the ciborium on the corporal, without blessing it or raising it.

The Assistant takes the wine and water to fill the chalices. He returns them to the acolyte. The Assistant does not bless or raise the chalices.

If the Peace is to be exchanged, the servers receive it from the President. The acolytes may then take it to members of the congregation, perhaps the person on the end of each row. They then return to the sanctuary.

See page 12 for detailed discussion of the Peace.

If the first part of the service has been at the chancel step, the President and his assistants now go to the sanctuary and take up the positions in diagram i.

The acolytes bring from the credence table to the altar the chalices, each with a pall and one with purificator and corporal.

See page 14 for detailed discussion of the Offertory.

One acolyte receives the collection and hands it to the Assistant.

The other acolyte receives the bread (in a ciborium or ciboria) and hands it to the Assistant.

If the ciborium contains small wafers, there should nevertheless be one priest's wafer added, or else this may be brought to the altar from the credence table on a paten.

The first acolyte receives the wine and water (the stoppers having been removed before the procession) and stands before the altar with them.

33 The president may praise God for his gifts in appropriate words to which all respond
Blessed be God for ever.

34 The offerings of the people may be collected and presented. These words may be used.
Yours, Lord, is the greatness ...

35 At the preparation of the gifts A HYMN may be sung.

The Assistant steps to the right and the President resumes his place at the centre. He may then say immediately (and quietly if the hymn is still being sung) the Offertory prayers (33) or sentence (34). Or else he may wait until the hymn has ended and then say the prayers or sentence aloud. Or they may be omitted altogether. After the prayers or sentence (or, if they are omitted, as soon as the President returns to the centre) he bows to those who have formed the Offertory procession. They bow to him and return to their places. The President may then wash his hands.

The Eucharistic Prayer
THE TAKING OF THE BREAD AND CUP AND THE GIVING OF THANKS

36 The president takes the bread and cup into his hands and replaces them on the holy table.

When the hymn has ended, the President silently lifts the elements a few inches above the altar and replaces them.

If there are several ciboria and chalices the Assistant may share this with him.

37 The president uses one of the four EUCHARISTIC PRAYERS which follow.

The President stands with hands extended throughout.

The acolyte places the remaining wine and water on the credence table. The acolytes go to their positions at either end of the altar.

The ciborium and chalices remain uncovered until after the Communion of the people, except that if a second chalice is to remain on the altar unused for part of the administration, it may be covered before the administration begins. See page 15 for text of Offertory prayers.

The crucifer comes forward with the lavabo, for the washing of the President's hands. He then goes to his position (see diagram i).

Throughout the Eucharistic Prayer the acolytes hold high their candles.

See page 16 for detailed discussion of the Eucharistic Prayer. Even if the people kneel for it, those in the sanctuary stand throughout.

All may bow at 'Holy, holy, holy Lord, God of power and might'.

(Eucharistic Prayer 1:)
... and unite us in the body of your
    Son,
Jesus Christ our Lord.
✠ Through him and ✠ with him, and
    ✠ in him,
by the power of the Holy Spirit,
with all who stand before you in
    earth and heaven,
we worship you, Father almighty,
in songs of everlasting praise:

All **Blessing and honour and glory**
        and power
     be yours for ever and ever.
     Amen.

At the name of Jesus the President joins
his hands and bows.

He makes the sign of the cross once or
three times over the elements.

He elevates the ciborium and chalice; or
he elevates the ciborium only and the
Assistant elevates the chalice.

The elements are placed again on the
altar.

The President and Assistant reverence the
elements.

Silence may be kept.

If the people have been standing for the
Eucharistic Prayer, the President may
now invite them to kneel.

The Communion
THE BREAKING OF THE BREAD
AND THE GIVING OF THE BREAD
AND CUP

42 THE LORD'S PRAYER is said
either as follows or in its traditional
form.
President As our Saviour taught
        us,
        so we pray.
All   **Our Father in heaven ...**

43 The president breaks the consecrated bread, saying
We break this bread ...

The Assistant may help with the Fraction
if there are many wafers to be broken.

44 Either here or during the distribution one of the following
anthems may be said.
Lamb of God ...

50

In Rite B other manual actions at the
words of Institution are ordered. In other
forms of the Eucharistic Prayer:

through Jesus Christ our Lord,
 ✠ by whom, and ✠ with whom, and ✠
  in whom,
in the unity of the Holy Spirit,
all honour and glory be yours, almighty
  Father,
(from all who stand before you in earth
  and heaven,)
now and for ever. **Amen.**

The servers replace their candles on or
near the altar.

The servers remain standing.

See page 17 for detailed discussion of the
Fraction.

The *Agnus Dei* covers the Fraction which
may take some time. Even with Series 3,
Agnus Dei (section 34) may be used at this
point.

45 Before the distribution the president says
Draw near with faith . . .

Additional words of invitation may be used (see section 85).

The President says this *before* he receives Communion.

46 The president and people receive the communion. At the distribution the minister says to each communicant
The body of Christ keep you . . .

Those who are to administer the chalice take it from the altar without any special ceremony.

47 During the distribution HYMNS and ANTHEMS may be sung.

48 If either or both of the consecrated elements be likely to prove insufficient, the president himself returns to the holy table and adds more, saying these words.
Father, giving thanks . . .

49 Any consecrated bread and wine which is not required for purposes of communion is consumed at the end of the distribution or after the service.

When all have communicated, the ciboria and chalices are returned to the altar or to the credence table and reverenced. The President and Assistant immediately consume what remains. This is best done at the credence but, if at the altar, in front of it, with their backs to the people. They then cover the ciboria and chalices and return to their positions behind the altar. They do not yet cleanse the vessels.

After Communion

50 AN APPROPRIATE SENTENCE may be said and A HYMN may be sung.

The sentence is said by the President or it could be sung by the choir.

If there is to be a long silence, the President and Assistant sit.

Servers	*Notes*
	The first of the people (probably the choir where there is one) approach the altar now.
The servers receive Communion standing with the President and Assistant round the altar. See page 19.	See page 18 for detailed discussion of the Giving of the Bread and Cup. If laymen are to assist with the administration, they come to the altar during the *Agnus Dei* or the words 'Draw near with faith' and receive Communion with the President and assistants around the altar.
After receiving Communion the servers reverence the elements. They then sit in their seats or stand in front of them.	
	The anthems may include the *Benedictus* and *Agnus Dei* if they have not been used before. Series 3 explicitly says so.
One of the servers should be alert to the need to bring more bread or wine to the altar.	
The servers return to stand in their positions in diagram i and reverence the elements when the President does so.	The people, who will have been kneeling, continue to do so until the hymn.
If there is to be a long silence, the servers should remain in their seats after the Communion and not return to their usual places until the President stands at the end of the silence.	Perhaps the best of the periods for silence. See page 25.

53

When the time of silence is over, the Assistant may announce the hymn. If it has not been done already, the Assistant takes the ciboria and chalices to the credence table and cleanses them with water. He leaves them on the credence table and returns to his place.

If the Dismissal is to be from the chancel step, when the crucifer and acolytes are in position, the President and Assistant, still behind the altar, bow to it, and the President may kiss it.

They then leave the sanctuary and follow the crucifer and acolytes in the procession.

51 Either or both of the following prayers or other suitable prayers are said (see section 86).

The President says these with hands extended.

If there is no lectern, the Assistant may hold a book for the President, if the procession has left the altar.

52 President Father of all . . .
   or

53 All   **Almighty God,
            we thank you . . .**

The Dismissal

54 The President may say this or an alternative BLESSING (section 77).

He should, if possible, memorise the blessing. He makes the sign of the cross at the Trinitarian name. But the Blessing may be omitted altogether.

55 President Go in peace to love and
             serve the Lord.
   All   **In the name of Christ.
             Amen.**

The President says this with hands extended.

Servers

The crucifer assists with the cleansing of the vessels.

If the Dismissal is to be from the chancel step, towards the end of the hymn the crucifer with the cross and the acolytes with the candles assemble before the altar facing east.

When the President has bowed to the altar, the crucifer and acolytes turn and move forward, stopping at a point near the people, facing west, where the President may say the Dismissal. They must so stand that the President can be clearly seen. Every church design will require something slightly different.

Notes

The people stand for the hymn. But in Series 3 this hymn (and the Ablutions and movements during it) follow the post-communion Prayers.

The people remain standing for the Prayers, and for the Dismissal which follows it.

For note on post-communion Prayers, see page 22.

or
President Go in the peace of
Christ.

All **Thanks be to God.**

From Easter Day to Pentecost
'Alleluia! Alleluia!' may be added
after both the versicle and the
response.

56 The ministers and people depart.

Without further reverence to the altar, the procession leaves either in this order (1) Crucifer and Acolytes; (2) Choir; (3) Assistant; (4) President; or, if there is a choir, it may follow the President if that is more convenient.

Appendix 2—Leading the Intercessions in the Eucharist: A Guide for the Laity

USING THE TEXT OF RITE A SECTION 21 (OR RITE B SECTION 18 OR SERIES 3 SECTION 10)

What Sort of Material Should You Include?

The set parts of the Intercessions printed in the text are *general* intercessions, praying rather vaguely for unity in the Church, justice in the world, *etc.* Your task is to give these some 'meat' by introducing specific intercessions, normally short sharp petitions which can be summed up in the set passages. It is better to avoid general inexact petitions that simply duplicate what the set text already says.

What Sources Should You Draw on for Subjects for Intercession?

Five obvious sources present themselves:

1. Your parish priest will very probably give you some sort of list, perhaps including a particular area of the world-wide Church to pray for, perhaps the name of the newly baptised or married, the sick, and the departed.

2. Look at your Parish Magazine or newsletter. See whether there is any event in the life of the parish in the coming week for which you should pray—a meeting of the Parochial Church Council for instance. Or, if there has been some major parish event, you may want to include a thanksgiving for that.

3. Consult your newspaper and watch the news on the television. National papers and television always provide material—events or situations which people will know about and want to pray about. Where you fear you may be accused of unwarranted political bias, don't just avoid the controversial subject, because the more fearful you are of

being misunderstood, the more likely it is a subject uppermost in people's minds—a crippling national strike or something similar. But certainly you do have to avoid suggesting political solutions. Best simply to pray for all those caught up in the situation asking that they may be given wisdom to discern the right solution. The *local* newspaper should also be consulted. Local issues need praying for as much as national ones.

4. Find out from your priest the theme of the Sunday. The readings and the sermon probably have a common idea running through them which can also find a place in the Intercessions or even form the basis of them.

5. Include your own special interests. Everyone asked to lead the Intercessions has his or her own special interests or expertise. Don't hesitate to bring these into the Intercessions. Without such variety they can become stereotyped. But there is one danger to avoid: because it is a subject you know a great deal about, it may be tempting to turn the Intercessions into a lecture or sermon to put people in the picture. Keep it brief!

How Should You Set About Presenting the Material?

The Different Sections
The prayer normally divides into five sections—1, The Church; 2, The World; 3, The Local Community; 4, The Suffering; 5, The Departed. The saints, if any are to be named, belong in 5, not in 1. If we pray for ourselves, this normally goes in 1, because we are the Church, or in 3, if it is a very local concern. The usual pattern in Rite A is the same as Rite B and Series 3. Your words in each section are followed by (a) silence, (b) the set text and (c) the versicle and response, 'Lord, in your mercy hear our prayer'. But in Rite A, you may (if it is your parish custom) reverse the order and place the versicle and response before the part of the set text that sums up the section. With A you may also divide the last two paragraphs, ((a) departed and (b) the whole Church including the saints), which seem to belong together as one section, into two when it seems appropriate. In the sections for the Suffering and the Departed your own words and the set text may be more closely

interwoven ('Comfort and heal all those who suffer in body, mind, or spirit...; give them courage', 'Hear us as we remember those who have died in the faith of Christ...; according to your promises'). But, as in B and 3, you still have the option to complete your own contribution before beginning the set text if that seems to make the prayer run more smoothly.

Talking to God

Remember that the prayer is addressed *to God*, not to the people. The form 'Let us pray for...' is therefore quite wrong because that is addressing the people. There are really two possible ways of writing the Intercession (and it is as well not to mix the two). The first is to begin each clause with the word 'we', so that each petition begins something like 'We pray to you for...', 'We remember before you...', 'We bring to you...' or 'We ask you...'. Alternatively each clause can begin with an *imperative* (just as the set parts do: Strengthen, Give, Comfort, and Heal). This is more difficult because you have to look for a variety of imperatives, else you will be constantly overusing the same few. But, if well done, this is a very effective style. It is brief and crisp. 'Uphold those who resist injustice' is more effective than 'We pray to you for those who resist injustice' and briefer too. If this form is used, there are many more suitable imperatives than you might at first think. 'Bless' is the most obvious one, but also 'Send your Holy Spirit to', 'Enlighten', 'Give Grace to', 'Help us to', 'Hear our prayer for', 'Have mercy on', 'Receive our thanks for' and many more.

You and Thou

Note that in Rite B God is addressed as 'Thou'. You should try to avoid mixing 'you' and 'thou' and 'your' and 'thy'. If you feel it difficult to write in a slightly archaic form and you feel you must use 'you' and 'your', rather than 'thou', 'thee' and 'thy', then you should carry that to its logical conclusion and change every 'thy' in the set text of the Intercessions to 'your'. One form or other throughout should be the aim. In Rite A and Series 3 there is no problem. God is addressed as 'you' throughout.

60

Starting Each Section
The first section, that for the Church, has already begun
'Almighty God . . .', so you come in half way through the
sentence with 'we pray for' or 'bless' or something similar. In
the other sections you are starting a sentence and therefore it is
quite a good idea to begin all of these sections with the word
'Father' or 'Lord'. The first sentence of each section should be
general because it is telling people what they are about to pray
for. So something general like 'Send your Holy Spirit upon
your Church' will be followed immediately by more specific
petitions.

Including other prayers
It is hardly ever a good thing to introduce chunks of prayers
you have found somewhere else, partly because they tend to be
general and simply duplicate what the set part of the
Intercessions says but also because they tend to be written in a
slightly different style and therefore don't quite fit. Of course
there will be occasional phrases you know from elsewhere that
you will want to use, but larger chunks, whole clauses and
sentences or even complete collects really don't fit. It's *your*
words that are most likely to convey the meaning you want to
get across.

Thanksgivings
The prayer is chiefly one of Intercession, asking for things. But,
on occasions, it will be sensible to put in thanksgivings, 'We
thank you for . . .' or 'Receive our thanks for . . .'. Use this only
sparingly because the great 'Thanksgiving' comes later in the
service.

Silence
Don't forget that the rubrics allow for silence in each section.
Don't prepare so much material that you feel obliged to omit
the periods of silence. People appreciate a few seconds to add
silently their own petitions.

Using a Theme
Certain days in the year call out for rather special treatment.
On the great festivals you will want the Intercessions to reflect
the matter being celebrated. Possibly each section can be linked

with the theme. For instance, at Ascensiontide the five sections might begin thus:

1. Jesus your Son is king. We your people pledge ourselves to work for the fullness of his Kingdom on earth. May your Church wait patiently and expectantly for every fresh manifestation of your Holy Spirit to give it new life and vision . . .

2. Father, Jesus your Son is king and it is your will to restore all things in him. Make all the nations subject to his just and gentle rule . . .

3. Father, may Jesus your Son reign in the heart of each one of us . . .

4. Father, Jesus your Son returned to you bearing all the weight of the world. So, with him, we bring to you all those in special need . . .

5. Father, Jesus your Son has gone before us to prepare a place for us. For where he is we are to be also. Welcome into your Kingdom all who have left this world in your friendship . . . .

A Specimen Form of Intercession

Rite A

Almighty God, our heavenly Father, who promised through your Son Jesus Christ to hear us when we pray in faith:

We pray for your Church throughout the world. Heal its divisions. Restore its unity. Empower its witness. Strengthen your Church in every land and particularly today hear our prayer for the church in Z and for its witness among all the political uncertainties of that area. And strengthen too the resolve of Christians caught up in the violence and tension of Y.

Strengthen A our bishop and all your Church in the service of Christ: that all who confess your name may be united in your truth, live together in your love, and reveal your glory to the world.

Lord, in your mercy

Hear our prayer.

Father: we pray for the world which your Church is called to serve. Bring your peace and justice where now there is war or tension or inequality. Have mercy upon the divided peoples of V and U. Inspire the leaders of our own nation, particularly those who influence our economic and industrial life. Strengthen the resolve of those who deal with increasing racial tension in our cities and restrain the forces of evil and prejudice.

Bless and guide Elizabeth our Queen; give wisdom to all in authority; and direct this and every nation in the ways of justice and of peace; that men may honour one another, and seek the common good.

Lord, in your mercy

Hear our prayer.

Rite B

Almighty God, who hast promised to hear the prayers of those who ask in faith:

We pray for thy Church throughout the world. Heal its divisions. Restore its unity. Empower its witness. Inspire its leaders, especially our bishop A. Strengthen thy Church in every land and particularly today hear our prayer for the church in Z and for its witness among all the political uncertainties of that area. And strengthen too the resolve of Christians caught up in the violence and tension of Y.

Grant that we who confess thy Name may be united in thy truth, live together in thy love, and show forth thy glory in the world.

Lord, in thy mercy

Hear our prayer.

Father: we pray for the world which thy Church is called to serve. Bring thy peace and justice where now there is war or tension or inequality. Have mercy upon the divided peoples of V and U. Inspire the leaders of our nation, particularly those who influence our economic and industrial life. Strengthen the resolve of those who deal with increasing racial tension in our cities and restrain the forces of evil and prejudice.

Give wisdom to all in authority, bless Elizabeth our Queen, and direct this nation and all nations in the ways of justice and of peace, that men may honour one another, and seek the common good.

Lord, in thy mercy

Hear our prayer.

Father: we pray for this local community and those who bear office within it. Give refreshment to all those now on holiday and keep them safe. Be with the church in this parish and guide us in all that we do in your name. Bless today all the people who live in *X* Road and all those associated with the *W* School, whether as teachers, pupils, managers or parents. Bless the *three* babies baptised here last Sunday—*C*, *D* and *E*—and make their homes Christian and loving. Bless *F* and *G*, married here yesterday, and strengthen them in their lives together.

Give grace to us, our families and friends, and to all our neighbours; that we may serve Christ in one another, and love as he loves us.

Lord, in your mercy

Hear our prayer.

Father: we pray for those in any sort of need. Give your strength to all families now coping with unemployment and to all school leavers without work. Be with all who suffer especially within our parish *HI, JK* and *LM*.

Comfort and heal all those who suffer in body, mind or spirit; give them courage and hope in their troubles; and bring them the joy of your salvation.

Lord, in your mercy

Hear our prayer.

Father: hear us as we remember those who have died in the faith of Christ. Give light and joy and fulfilment to them, and especially to *OP* and *QR* who died this week. According to your promises, grant us with them a share in your eternal kingdom.

Rejoicing in the fellowship of *N* and of all your saints, we commend ourselves and all Christian people to your unfailing love.

Merciful Father,

Father, we pray for this local community and those who bear office within it. Give refreshment to all those now on holiday and keep them safe. Be with the church in this parish and guide us in all that we do in thy name. Bless today all the people who live in *X* Road and all those associated with the *W* School, whether as teachers, pupils, managers or parents. Bless the *three* babies baptised here last Sunday—*C*, *D* and *E*—and make their homes Christian and loving. Bless *F* and *G*, married here yesterday, and strengthen them in their lives together.

Give grace to us, our families, and friends, and to all our neighbours in Christ, that we may serve him in one another, and love as he loves us.

Lord, in thy mercy

Hear our prayer.

Father, we pray for those in any sort of need of body, mind or spirit. Give thy strength to all families now coping with unemployment and to all school leavers without work. Give courage and hope to all who suffer, especially within our parish to *HI, JK* and *LM*.

Save and comfort those who suffer, that they may hold to thee through good and ill, and trust in thy unfailing love.

Lord, in thy mercy

Hear our prayer.

Father: receive our thanks for the example of *N*, whose festival we have kept this week, and for all thy saints and martyrs. Give light and joy and fulfilment to all who have died, especially to *OP* and *QR* who died this week.

Hear us as we remember those who have died in faith, and grant us with them a share in thy eternal kingdom.

Merciful Father,

accept these prayers
for the sake of your Son,
our Saviour Jesus Christ. Amen.

accept these prayers
for the sake of thy Son,
our Saviour Jesus Christ. Amen.